kidpower

children's safety comics

COLOR EDITION

Use your power to stay safe!

Irene van der Zande
Illustrated by Amanda Golert

A publication of Kidpower Teenpower Fullpower International

Copyright and Permission To Use Information

Copyright Information
Kidpower® Children's Safety Comics Color Edition. © 2010, 2018, 2020, 2021. All content in this book is copyrighted to author Irene van der Zande, Kidpower Teenpower Fullpower International founder and executive director. No part of this publication may be reproduced in any form or by any electronic or mechanical means, including information and retrieval systems, without prior written permission of the author or her designated representative.

Reproduction Information
Prior written permission must be obtained for reproducing any part of this publication in any form. However, a wealth of resources including some articles and handouts from this book are available for free on the Kidpower.org website. For information about how to obtain permission for different kinds of content use, please visit www.kidpower.org or contact the author at safety@kidpower.org.

Use of Content for Personal Learning or for Teaching Others
With proper acknowledgment, readers are encouraged to use knowledge from the Kidpower Teenpower Fullpower programs about self-protection, confidence-building, advocacy, personal safety, positive communication, child protection, leadership, team-building, bullying prevention, child abuse prevention, positive youth development, and self-defense strategies and skills in their personal lives and professional activities.

We ask that readers tell people about Kidpower Teenpower Fullpower International when they use any examples, ideas, stories, language, and/or practices that they learned from our program, and let others know how to reach our organization.

Please note that permission to use content from our copyrighted programs verbally and in person is **not** permission to publish or duplicate any part of this content in any written or digital form in print or online, including in articles, lesson plans, research papers, newsletters, books, videos, podcasts, websites, etc. These uses require separate permission as described above.

Restrictions
Unless people or agencies have an active agreement with Kidpower Teenpower Fullpower International, they are not authorized to represent themselves or give the appearance of representing themselves as working under our organization's auspices. This means that individuals and groups must have an active certification or agreement with our organization to be authorized to teach, promote, or organize workshops or other presentations using the Kidpower, Teenpower, Fullpower program names, workshop names, reputation, or credentials. Please visit www.kidpower.org or e-mail safety@kidpower.org about our instructor certification, authorized provider, and center development programs.

Liability Disclaimer
Each situation is unique, and we can make no guarantee about the safety or effectiveness of the content or techniques described in this material. We do not accept liability for any negative consequences from use of this material.

Kidpower Teenpower Fullpower International
Office: 831-426-4407 or (USA) 1-800-467-6997
E-mail: safety@kidpower.org   Web page: www.kidpower.org
Address: P.O. Box 1212, Santa Cruz, CA 95061, USA

Table of Contents

FOR ADULTS
Getting Started - For Caring Adults 4
How To Use This Book..................5
How Adults Can Help Kids Stay Safe 6
More Ways Adults Can Help Kids Stay Safe 7
Kidpower's Founding Principle: Put Safety FIRST!........8
Make The Kidpower Protection Promise™ 9

FOR CHILDREN AND ADULTS
Be Aware, Calm, Respectful, And Confident 10
Different Kinds Of Power..................11
Leaving To Stop Problems 12
Walk Away Power 13
Together Or On Your Own 14
Where Is Safety? 15
Checking First To Be Safe..................16
The Pizza Story 17
What Is A Stranger?..................18
Checking First Rules With Strangers 19
More Times To Check First 20
The Kid At The Park 21
How Can A Stranger Know Your Name?..................22
Getting Help In Emergencies 23
Your Safety Plan If You Are Lost In A Store 24
When To Wait And When To Interrupt 25
Yell, Leave, And Get Help If You Are Scared 26
The Big Kid Being Scary 27
Introduction To Boundaries 28
The Bath Story..................29
The Trash Can For Hurting Words 30
Taking In Compliments 31
The 'I Don't Like You' Story 32
The 'Stupid Crybaby' Story 33
Saying Kind Words To Ourselves 34
More Ways To Be Kind To Ourselves 35
Kidpower Consent Checklist 36
Choice And Not A Choice 37
The Kisses Story 38
Safety With Touch Means You Can Always Tell 39
How To Stop Unwanted Touch 40
Fun Surprises And Unsafe Secrets 41
What Is A Bribe? 42
Kidpower Safety Rules About Private Areas 43
The Hot Day..................44
The Sleepover 45
The 'Uh Oh' Feeling 46
The Curiosity Story 47
Keep Telling Until You Get Help 48
The Busy Mom Story 49
The Tired Grandpa Story 50
'People Safety' Skills To Stop Bullying 51
More Ways To Stop Bullying 52
Tattling And Telling – What's The Difference? 53
Kyle Stays Safe With His Body 54
Safety With Cars 55
The Big Sister 56
Kidpower Safety Signals for Everyone, Everywhere To Help Prevent And Solve Problems 57
Kidpower Safety Signals For Taking Charge Of Our Feelings, Words, And Bodies 58
Kidpower Safety Signals For Building Better Relationships 59
Kidpower Safety Signals For Taking Charge Of Our Safety 60
Kidpower Safety Signals For Healthy Boundaries With People We Know..................61
Best Friends and Mistakes..................62

MORE FOR ADULTS
Discussions And Practices To Build Understanding And Skills 64
Kidpower Services For All Ages And Abilities 72
Recommended Kidpower Curriculum Books 73
Online Kidpower Resources 74
Acknowledgments 75
About The Author 76
About The Illustrator and Featured Contributor 76

Getting Started - For Caring Adults

Adult leadership is essential for keeping kids safe. Pages 4 to 9 and pages 64 to 71 are for YOU! This information for parents, teachers, and other caring adults describes how to protect children and how to support them in learning, practicing, and using these 'People Safety' strategies, safety rules, and skills in daily life. The *Safety Signals* the *Best Friends and Mistakes Story* and on pages 57 to 63 are for both adults and kids.

We use the term 'People Safety' to mean knowledge and skills for preventing and solving problems with people. Fire Safety means much more than 'burning prevention' – it also means being able to use fire safely for warmth, cooking, and fun. In the same way, a strong foundation of 'People Safety' skills does much more than preventing problems like bullying and abuse – 'People Safety' is also important for developing healthy relationships that add joy and meaning to our lives.

Starting on page 10, we have entertaining drawings, clear explanations, and social stories for children ages 3 to 10 who are usually with adults, such as parents or teachers, who can help them if they have a safety problem. These skills, ideas, and teaching methods are also important for toddlers and teenagers—and for their adults.

Here are some tips for how to prepare kids to take charge of their safety in ways that are effective and emotionally safe:

1. **Make learning about safety an ongoing process rather than a one-time lesson.** Talking about the bad things that can happen can create anxiety, without making kids safer. Practicing what to say and do in ways that are fun helps to reduce anxiety, build confidence, and increase competence.

2. **Kids learn more from what they see and are successful doing than from what you tell them.** Set a good example by using our 'Put Safety First' Founding Principle on page 8 in daily life. Notice and focus on what kids are doing right instead of paying attention mostly to the ways you want them to change. Use the *Discussions and Practices* section on pages 64 to 71 to act out the skills that are shown in the stories.

3. **Make SURE kids know you care.** Children are safest when they know they have caring adults in their lives who believe in them and who they can trust to help them when they have a problem. Discuss the *Kidpower Protection Promise* on page 9. Ask children calmly, "Is there anything you have been worrying or wondering about?" Listen to their answers respectfully without lecturing or joking, and thank them for telling you. Tell them often, "I love you just the way you are."

Kidpower teaches kids to use their power to stay safe!

How To Use This Book

Discuss and practice these ideas with your family, school, or youth group so that everyone has a common understanding about safety.

1. Read the book yourself. Notice how many of these ideas and skills are important for adults too.

2. Discuss the relevant sections of the book with your children. Point out the different ways that children in the stories are solving a variety of 'People Safety' problems.

3. Follow the *Discussion and Practices* directions on pages 64 to 71 to practice the skills together.

4. Remember to use these skills out in the real world every day.

How Adults Can Help Kids Stay Safe

Stay calm and in charge. Plan ahead by making and practicing safety plans together.

1. Stay calm. Children learn better when their grown-ups are calm.

2. Stay in charge. Children need adult supervision and protection in person and online until they have enough skills and life experience to take charge of their own safety.

3. Make a **Safety Plan** for how to get help everywhere you go. The Safety Plan will be different for different people, at different times of the day, and in different places.

4. Review and practice 'People Safety' skills every day, everywhere. Read the *Best Friends and Mistakes Story* on pages 62 to 63 to help children think about making safe choices and getting help.

More Ways Adults Can Help Kids Stay Safe

Kids learn more from *what they do* and from *what they see their adults doing* than from what they are told to do.

1. Help children be **successful** in practicing skills by **coaching** them to handle problems in the moment.

2. Help children **understand** about strangers. Tell them most people are good. If they do not know someone well, their **Safety Plan** is to **Check First** with you right away.

3. **Set a good example.** Solve problems respectfully and powerfully.

4. When you **listen** to children and **respect** their feelings, they are **more likely** to come to you when they need help.

Kidpower's Founding Principle: Put Safety FIRST!

The safety and wellbeing of young people – and adults – are more important than anyone's embarrassment, inconvenience, or offense. Make a commitment to Put Safety First in daily life.

Make The kidpower Protection Promise

Imagine the impact if all caring adults discuss this message with
all of the young people in our lives - and show them that we mean it!

You are VERY important to me!
If you have a safety problem, I want to know.
Even if I seem too busy.
Even if someone we care about will be upset.
Even if it is embarrassing.
Even if you promised not to tell.
Even if you made a mistake.
Please tell me, and I will do everything in my power to help you.

BE AWARE, CALM, RESPECTFUL, AND CONFIDENT

People will **bother you less and listen to you more** when you are looking around; acting calm, respectful, and confident; and staying in control of your body.

1. Stuart is not paying attention and looks scared. This is **less safe**.

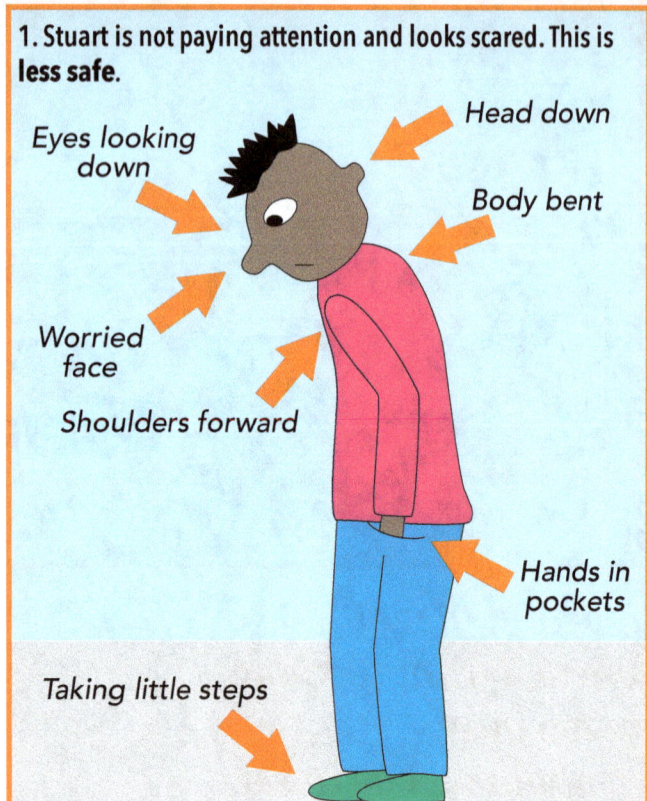

- Eyes looking down
- Head down
- Body bent
- Worried face
- Shoulders forward
- Hands in pockets
- Taking little steps

2. Stuart looks aware and strong. This is **more safe**.

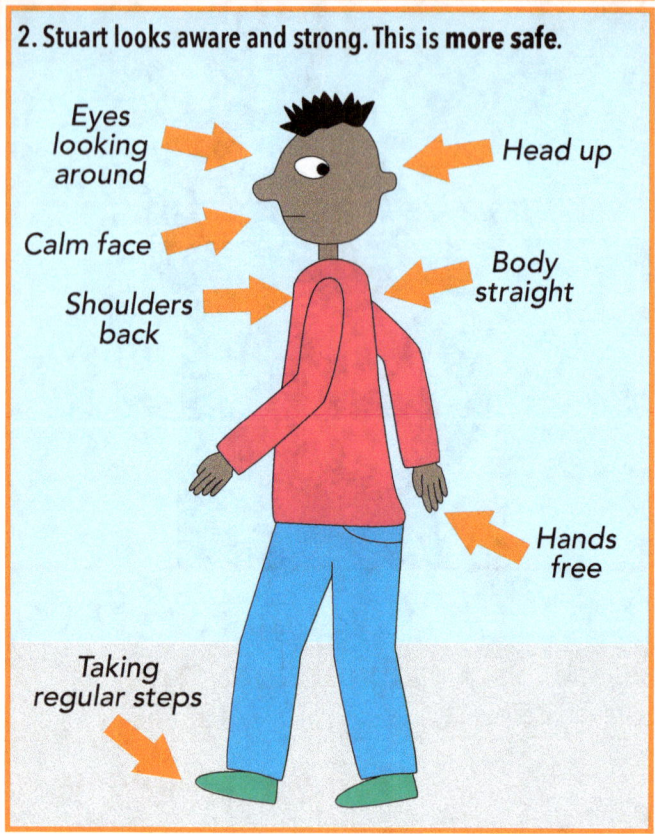

- Eyes looking around
- Head up
- Calm face
- Body straight
- Shoulders back
- Hands free
- Taking regular steps

3. Mariah is very angry. She looks like she wants to fight. This is **less safe**.

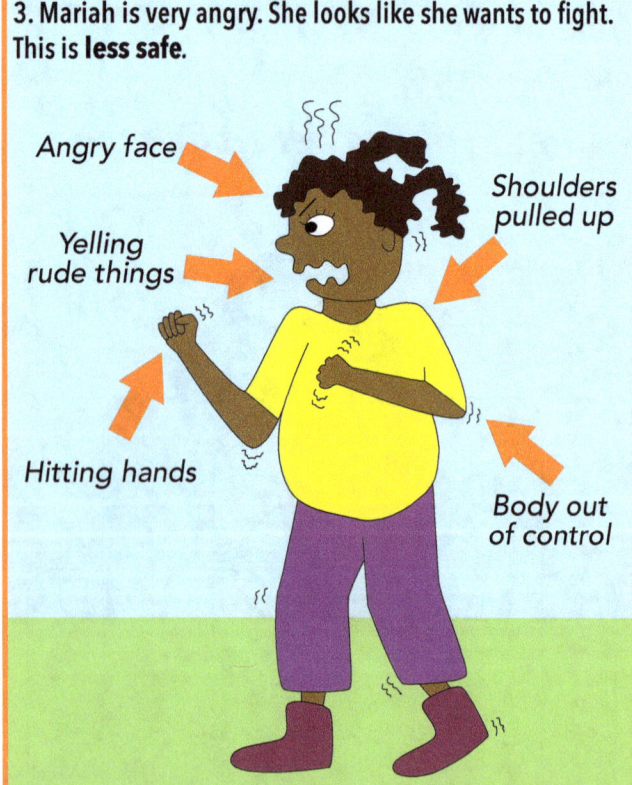

- Angry face
- Shoulders pulled up
- Yelling rude things
- Hitting hands
- Body out of control

4. No matter how she feels inside, Mariah acts calm, confident, and respectful.

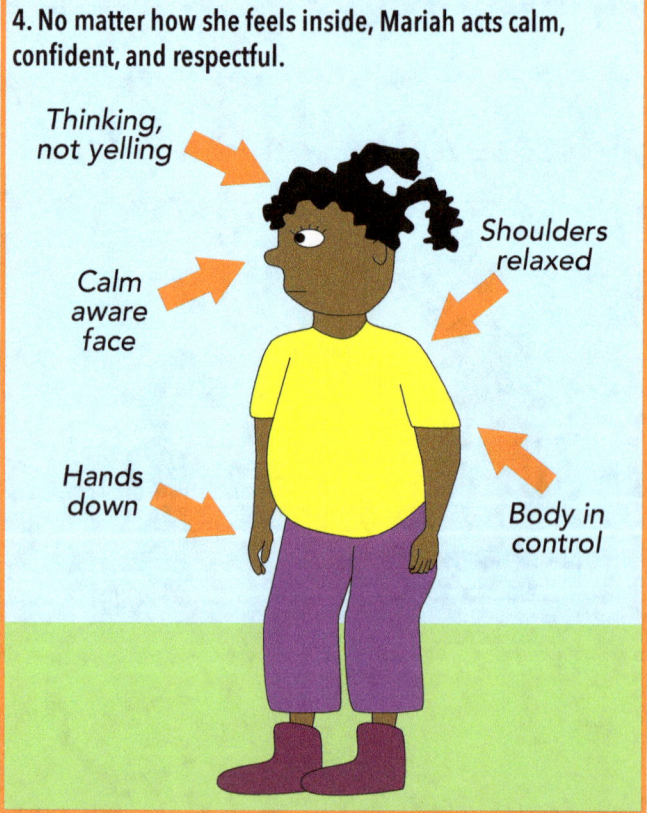

- Thinking, not yelling
- Shoulders relaxed
- Calm aware face
- Hands down
- Body in control

DIFFERENT KINDS OF POWER
We have the power to make safe choices.

1. Rana is rude and sticks out her tongue. Peter keeps his tongue and words in his mouth by using his **Mouth Closed Power** to stay safe.

2. Eric hits his big brother. His big brother stops the hit and uses his **Hands Down Power** to keep himself from hitting back.

3. Nancy tries to grab the scooter. Michael uses his **STOP! Power** by having a strong voice and making a fence with his hands so he sounds and looks like he means it.

4. George yells at his friend. His friend does *not* yell back. She uses her **Walk Away Power** to get away from George's hurtful words and to stay safe.

LEAVING TO STOP PROBLEMS

Moving out of reach helps to stop problems from growing bigger.

1. Michelle likes to play with her friend Yoko in the sandbox.

2. When Yoko gets mad and throws things, she can be mean to Michelle.

3. When Yoko is in a bad mood, Michelle can **walk away**.

4. Michelle can play with other children, or she can play by herself.

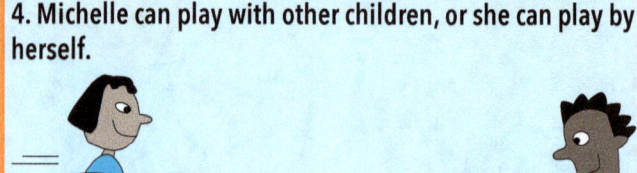

GUIDE FOR ADULTS: How to practice **Moving Out of Reach** with children

Make sure there is space behind child.

1. Coach the child to start close and facing you, then to back up slowly and split their attention by looking at you and glancing back to make sure there is nothing behind them.

Keep one foot in place

Make sure child has moved out of reach.

2. Check to see if the child is out of reach. Coach kids to be successful. Do not grab them if they are too close. Just coach them to move back more.

WALK AWAY POWER

It is not fun to be pushed when waiting in line. It is more important to be next to someone who is not pushing than to be at the front of the line.

1. Annabelle is pushing in line. Mariela has not done or said anything, but Annabelle is still bothering her.

2. Mariela wishes Annabelle would stop pushing. But Annabelle does not notice and pushes more.

3. Mariela gets mad and pushes back. The teacher tells both of them not to fight.

4. Next time Annabelle pushes, Mariela leaves her place in the line and finds another place. She would rather be next to a friendly kid who does not push than to stay near the front of the line and get pushed.

TOGETHER OR ON YOUR OWN

The **rules are different** if you are **together** with an adult who can help you or if you are **on your own**.

1. If Chris is right next to his mom at the store, **they are together**.

Together

2. A man at the store is giving out free samples. If Chris' mom gives permission, he can take food from the man.

Get Permission

3. If Chris and his mom are away from each other even a short time, Chris is **on his own**. If his mom is in the next aisle and a lady has free samples...

On Your Own

4. Chris' Safety Plan is to move away and go to his mom so he can **Check First**.

Move Away and Check First

CHECKING FIRST TO BE SAFE

One of the best ways to keep yourself safe is to **Check First** with your adults.

1. **Check First** with your adults before you play with animals unless you know them very well.

2. **Check First** with your adults before you get out of your car seat, unhook your seat belt, or get out of the car.

3. **Check First** with your adults before you go out the gate, out the door, or out of the house, even if something very interesting is happening.

4. Keep **Checking First** before you touch the stove, plug anything into an electric outlet, or use matches until your adults say it is safe.

THE PIZZA STORY

Even if you know someone well, **Check First before you change your plan** about where you are going, who is with you, and what you are doing.

1. Chen and his sister Lia are walking home after school.

2. Their Mom surprises them by driving up.

   "Hi kids! Let's get pizza!"
   "Yeah, pizza!"

3. Their Grandma is at home waiting for the kids. When they don't come home after school, she gets worried. She tries to figure out where they are.

4. Their Grandma calls the police. The police find her grandkids and their Mom at the pizza restaurant.

   "Hello, police. I am so worried. My grandkids aren't home, and I don't know where they are."

5. Grandma is very glad and very mad.

   "WHY DIDN'T YOU CALL ME?!"
   "I am sorry. We forgot. From now on, we will Check First before we change the plan."

6. Chen and Lia's neighbor invites them to come over. They've been at his house before, but they remember to **Check First before they change their plans**.

   "Your Mom says you can come over to my house for cookies."
   "We'd love to, and we need to Check First with Mom ourselves."

WHAT IS A STRANGER?

A stranger is just someone you don't know well. Strangers can look like anybody. **Most people are good**, and most strangers are good.

1. You don't have to worry about strangers. You just need to **Stay Together** and **Check First** with your adults.

2. You will often meet lots of strangers on the first day of a school or of a class.

3. No matter what people are wearing or look like, they are still strangers unless you really know them.

4. People you know a little are called acquaintances. Until you know them well, **Check First** with your adults.

CHECKING FIRST RULES WITH STRANGERS

Check First before you **get close** to a stranger, **talk to** a stranger, or **take anything** from a stranger, **even your own things**.

MORE TIMES TO CHECK FIRST

Check First so your adults know **who** is with you, **where** you are going, and **what** you are doing, especially with people you don't know well.

1. If someone you don't know tries to take your photo...

2. ...**Move Away** and **Check First!**

3. If someone else has an emergency – Check First!

4. If someone is wearing a uniform – Check First!

THE KID AT THE PARK

Your **Safety Plan** is to **Check First** with your adults before you change **your plan** about where you go and who is with you, even with another kid.

1. Ashton is playing at the park. He wishes he had a friend to play with. Can you play with another kid you don't know well? Of course! As long as you Check First!

2. Ashton is happy when a kid he likes wants to play. And he needs to let his grown-ups know before he plays a game like hide-and-seek.

3. Ashton asks the other kid to wait so he can go to his grown-ups and Check First.

4. Ashton's grown-ups tell him he can play as long as he stays inside the park fence and he comes right away when they call him.

HOW CAN A STRANGER KNOW YOUR NAME?

Even if someone looks familiar and knows your name, **Move Away and Check First** with your adults, unless you are sure you really know this person.

1. If someone calls out your name at the park or in another public place, all the strangers nearby can learn your name.

2. There are lots of ways we can learn someone's name without really knowing this person.

3. Maya is playing in the hall by her apartment. A stranger calls her name.

4. The stranger is nice, but Maya moves away.

5. Maya Checks First.

6. Maya's grown-up helps her.

GETTING HELP IN EMERGENCIES

If you have an **emergency and cannot Check First**, your Safety Plan is to **Get Help**, even from someone you don't know.

1. You can get help from paramedics.

2. You can get help from firefighters.

3. You can get help from a group searching for people who are lost.

4. If you are lost and need help, a safer choice might be to ask a woman with children.

© A publication of Kidpower Teenpower Fullpower International® www.kidpower.org For permission to copy, contact safety@kidpower.org

YOUR SAFETY PLAN IF YOU ARE LOST IN A STORE

When you go out in public, be sure to **ask your adults** about your **Safety Plan** if you get lost.

1. Everywhere you go, make a **Safety Plan** with your grown-up for what to do if you get lost.

2. The first thing to do is to stand tall and still. **Look around** to see if you can find your grown-up.

3. The next thing to do is **yell for your grown-up in a big, loud voice**.

4. If that does not work, go to the **front of the checkout line**, not the back. **Interrupt** the cashier and ask for help.

5. If the cashier does not understand, ask again and say that you are lost.

6. It is okay to tell the cashier your grown-up's name.

WHEN TO WAIT AND WHEN TO INTERRUPT

You might have to **wait** if you **want** something.
Interrupt and keep asking for help if there is a **safety problem**.

1. You **wait** when your adult is busy even if you want to talk.

2. You **interrupt** your adult when the pot is boiling over on the stove.

3. You **wait** when your adult is on the phone even if they have been talking forever.

4. You **interrupt** your adult when a kid is hurting another kid.

5. You go to the end of the line and **wait** your turn when you want to buy something in a store.

6. You go to the front of the line and **interrupt** the cashier to get help if you are lost in the store.

© A publication of Kidpower Teenpower Fullpower International® www.kidpower.org For permission to copy, contact safety@kidpower.org

YELL, LEAVE, AND GET HELP IF YOU ARE SCARED

You can use the power of your voice and body to get away and get to Safety.

1. A big kid pushes Jordan. He is scared.

2. Jordan yells, runs, and goes to his teacher for help.

3. A dog barks. Elise is scared.

4. Elise can tell the dog firmly to stop. She can back away and go to her mom for help.

5. Some kids on the playground are very angry. Jeremy is scared.

6. Jeremy yells, runs, and goes to the adult in charge for help.

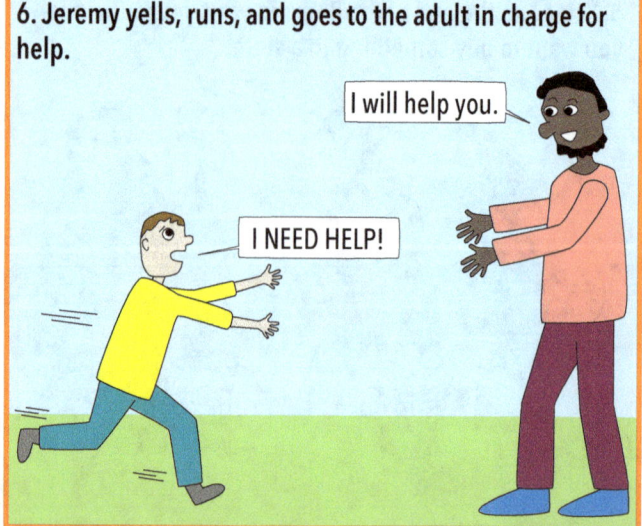

THE BIG KID BEING SCARY

If someone is acting unsafely, you can protect yourself by yelling in a strong voice and running to your adult to get help.

1. Brittany likes to go to the store with her mom.

2. A big kids grabs Brittany because he thinks it's funny, but she is scared.

3. Brittany pulls her arm away and yells.

4. She uses her **Stop Sign** and a **big voice** to surprise the big kid.

5. Brittany **runs and yells for help**.

6. Her mom helps her, and the big kid is sorry.

© A publication of Kidpower Teenpower Fullpower International® www.kidpower.org For permission to copy, contact safety@kidpower.org

INTRODUCTION TO BOUNDARIES

A boundary is like a fence. It sets a limit. Personal boundaries are the limits between people. Clear personal boundaries help us to have more fun and fewer problems with people.

The Kidpower Safety Rules about personal boundaries are:

1. **We each belong to ourselves.** You belong to you, and I belong to me. This means that your body belongs to you—and so does your personal space, your feelings, your time, your thoughts—all of you! This means that other people belong to themselves too.
2. **Some things are not a choice.** This is true for adults as well as kids. Especially for kids, touch for health and safety is often not a choice.
3. **Problems should not be secrets.** Anything that bothers you, me, or anybody else should not have to be a secret, even if telling makes someone upset or embarrassed. Also, presents, photos, videos, games, activities, friendships, and any kind of touch should not have to be a secret.
4. **Keep telling until you get help.** When you have a problem, find adults you trust and keep telling until you get the help you need. It is never too late to tell.

1. We each belong to ourselves.

2. Some things are not a choice.

3. Problems should not be secrets.

4. Keep telling until you get help.

THE BATH STORY

This story shows how the boundary rules can work in real life.

1. Sometimes Indira does not want to take a bath.

2. Her Mom says she has to take a bath to be clean and healthy.

3. Indira can tell everyone that she is angry that she had to have a bath.

4. India's Mom was right to say that Indira could tell anyone about the bath. Suppose she had said, "Oh, you must NOT tell. It's too embarrassing!" Saying that would have been a safety mistake, because problems should not be secrets.

THE TRASH CAN FOR HURTING WORDS

If people say hurting words to you, **protect your feelings.**
Throw the hurting words away, and say something kind to yourself.

1. Sharon uses her Kidpower Trash Can instead of taking hurting words inside her body or her mind.

2. Sharon puts her hand on her hip and imagines the hole her arm makes is her Kidpower Trash Can. She catches the hurting word 'Stupid' and throws it away.

3. Sharon can also throw hurting words into a real trash can and put kind words into her heart.

4. Sometimes friends can use mean words. Louis uses his Kidpower Trash Can to throw away 'Weirdo'.

5. Anna makes a Trash Can with her mind.

6. Heidi uses her Trash Can when she says something mean to herself.

TAKING IN COMPLIMENTS

Compliments are kind words that help you feel good about yourself. When someone gives you a compliment, take it inside your heart, and say, "Thank you!"

1. Latisha likes what her little sister built. Her little sister throws the compliment away.

2. Latisha tells her again. She wants her little sister to believe the compliment.

3. Kyle tells his older brother that he looks cool. His big brother throws the compliment away.

4. Kyle tries again because he wants his big brother to take good words into his heart, not throw them away.

THE 'I DON'T LIKE YOU' STORY

Learning to protect your feelings from hurting words can help you to feel good about yourself instead of bad about yourself.

1. When Sharona's friend suddenly gets into a bad mood, she says mean words. If Sharona does not protect herself, the hurting words can feel like they are going like an arrow into her heart.

2. Sharona tries to make herself forget what her friend said, but the hurting words feel stuck inside her heart and her head.

3. Sharona can protect her feelings by catching the hurting words instead of letting them come inside.

4. She can throw the hurting words into her Kidpower Trash Can and say something nice to herself. She can find another friend or go to an adult for help.

THE 'STUPID CRYBABY' STORY

Crying can help you feel better! Grown-ups cry too. If someone cries, be kind.

1. Steve feels sad, angry, and embarrassed when some kids call him unkind names. It is normal to get upset when people say hurtful things.

2. When Steve says mean things back to these kids, he gets into a big argument that turns into a fight. Fights are not safe, and everyone gets into trouble.

3. When other kids say mean things, Steve can make a safety decision to use his Kidpower Trash Can to protect his feelings. He throws the hurting words away.

4. Steve uses his Heart Power to say something kind to himself. He does not get into a fight or into trouble. He keeps his feelings AND his body safe. Later, he discusses what happened with an adult he trusts.

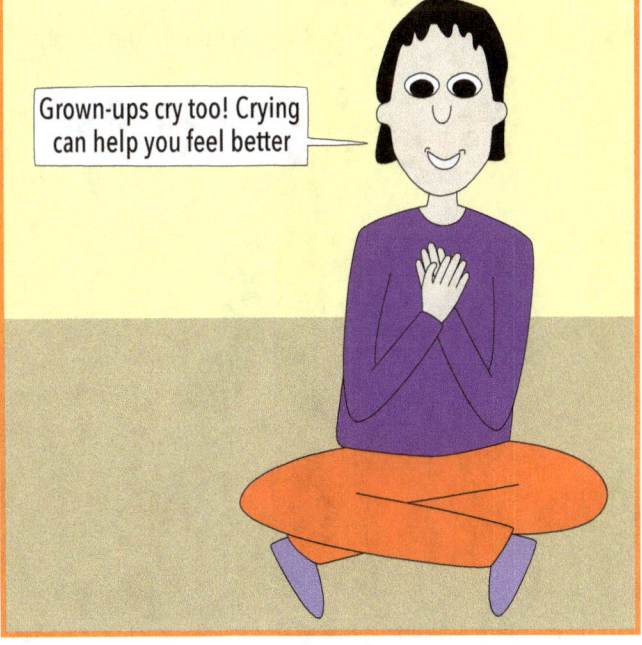

SAYING KIND WORDS TO OURSELVES

We do **not** have to be perfect to be GREAT! Throw away mean things you say to yourself and use **Positive Self-Talk** to be safe in your thoughts and feelings.

1. Learning new things can be really hard sometimes. Edward is learning to write and is getting upset because he feels stuck.

2. Edward realizes that he is being unkind and unfair to himself. He throws away the words 'too hard' and 'I can't' and decides that, "When I feel stuck, it is time to ask for help."

3. Simon accidently drops a cup of hot chocolate on the floor. There is chocolate everywhere!

4. Simon decides to throw away the hurting words 'clumsy' and 'dumb' along with the paper towel he used to clean up the mess. And then he goes to get more hot chocolate.

MORE WAYS TO BE KIND TO OURSELVES

5. Ana feels angry with herself because she forgot to bring her library book back to school.

"Did everyone bring back your library book?"

"I am a **bad** person for forgetting my book!"

6. Ana realizes that everybody forgets things sometimes. Next time she'll make a plan to help herself remember to bring back her book.

"I am sorry. I will bring it with me tomorrow."

BAD PERSON

Mistakes are part of learning!

7. Irene is standing in front of the mirror, wishing she looked different. She thinks straight hair like her best friend has would look nicer – and be easier to take care of!

"Curly hair is **UGLY**! I wish I had straight hair like my friend!"

8. Irene decides to be kind to herself.

"It's okay to be different than my friend. My hair has its OWN way of looking good!"

The Kidpower Mini-Trash Can

9. Harry gets upset every time he makes a mistake. He feels like he keeps making the same mistakes over and over.

"HOW could I make such a STUPID mistake!"

10. Harry remembers to give himself positive messages. All of us need to remember that we do NOT have to be perfect to be GREAT!

"Mistakes are part of learning! I don't have to be perfect to be GREAT!"

STUPID MISTAKE

kidpower CONSENT CHECKLIST

Touch, attention, and games for play, affection, and fun should be the **choice** of each person, **safe**, **allowed** by the adults in charge, and **not a secret**.

1. Consent means touch or play for fun or affection are the **choice of each person**. In this example, both people and animals like this touch, so it is okay.

2. One person wants to tickle, and the other wants to stop. So it is not okay to keep tickling.

"Tickle tickle!"

"Stop that game. I don't like it!"

3. Touch or play for fun or affection should be safe.

4. Miguel and the baby are having fun, and holding a baby like this is **not** being safe. This touch is not okay because someone could get hurt.

"Be careful! That is NOT safe!"

5. Touch or play for fun or affection should be okay with the grown-ups in charge.

"Thank you for wiping her face."

6. This touch is **not** okay even though both kids are having fun and being safe. It is against the rules of the grown-ups in this house to play with food.

"NO playing with FOOD! That is NOT allowed!"

CHOICE AND NOT A CHOICE

Your body belongs to you, and some things are not a choice.

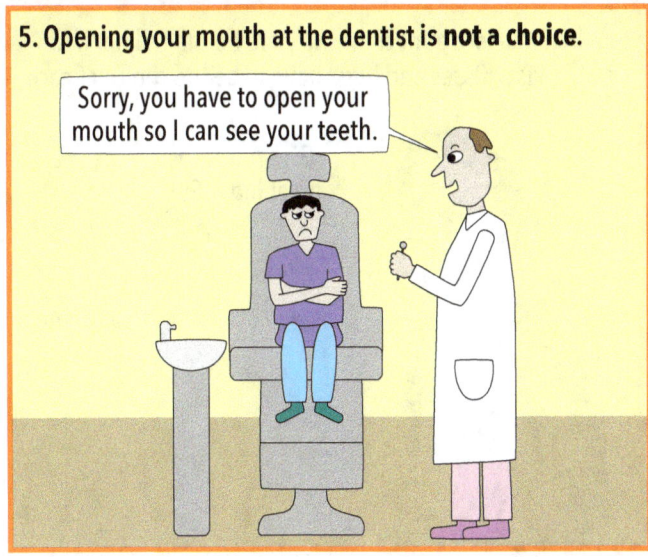

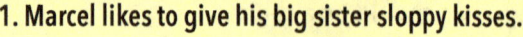

HOW TO STOP UNWANTED TOUCH

Consent means that touch is the **choice of both** people and you **can tell people to stop** unwanted touch.

1. If Kim likes it when her friend tickles her, that is fine.

2. Kim can **change her mind**. She uses her eyes, words, and body to tell her friend when she wants to stop.

3. If he **does not listen**, she can **stand up**, **move away**, **make a fence** with her hands, and say, "Stop!"

4. If her friend is **sad or mad** because Kim told him to stop, she can tell him that **she is sorry and he still has to stop**.

5. If Kim's friend tries to give her a treat so she will let him keep tickling, this is an **unsafe bribe**.

6. Even if Kim has to promise not to tell, **the safety rule is to go tell and keeping telling** until she gets help.

FUN SURPRISES AND UNSAFE SECRETS

Fun surprises are safe because **people will know** and they do **not break the Safety Rules**. Secrets about presents or treats someone gives you are not safe.

1. A surprise party or present for someone is a safe secret that the person being surprised will know about soon.

2. People who ask you to **keep treats or gifts a secret are making a safety mistake**.

3. Most grown-ups who care about you will understand.

4. Even if your grown-ups might be annoyed, it is still important to tell.

kidpower SAFETY RULES ABOUT PRIVATE AREAS

Understanding rules about private areas helps everybody be safe.
Anything about people and their private areas **should never have to be a secret.**

1. Private areas are the parts of the body that can be covered by a two-piece bathing suit.

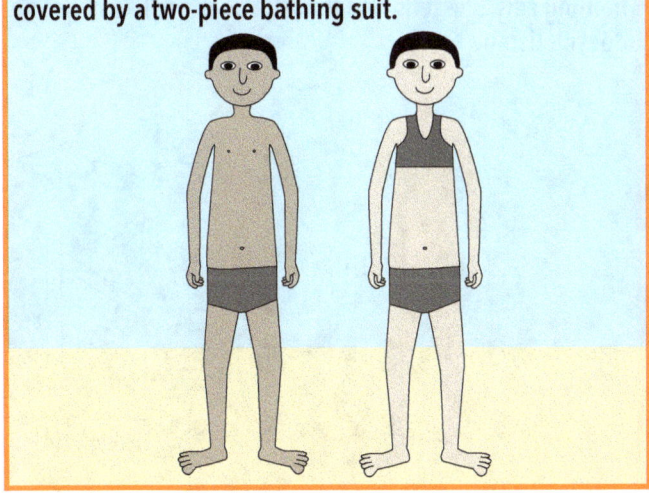

2. For play or teasing, other people should not touch your private areas. They should not ask you to touch their private areas either.

"Let's take off our clothes so we can play doctor!"

"That is against our safety rules. We can play doctor with our clothes on."

3. Sometimes grown-ups have to touch kids' private areas to help them.

"I need to put medicine on your sore."

4. Touch of any kind **should never ever be a secret.** You should always be able to talk about things you don't like.

"Mom put medicine on my bottom today! I did not like it."

"Thank you for telling me. I am sorry you didn't like it."

5. People should not show kids pictures or videos of people and their private areas.

"Look at these pictures of grown-ups."

"They don't have clothes on. Stop or will tell."

6. Even if the person stops, you should tell about anything that bothers you.

"My friend's brother tried to show me pictures on his computer of people touching their private areas. I said, 'Stop or I will tell.'"

"Thank you for telling me. We will help him understand about the safety rules."

THE HOT DAY

Games where someone tries to pull off the clothes of kids for fun or teasing are **not safe**.

1. It's a hot day. Carolina and her friend Jake are happy playing together in their little swimming pool and cooling off.

2. Jake thinks it's funny to try to pull off Carolina's bathing suit. She tells him that she does not like it, but he doesn't listen.

STOP!!!

HA HA HA!

3. Carolina follows her Safety Rules about private areas and tells their child care person that she needs help to get Jake to listen. Their adult is glad she is letting him know.

He keeps trying to pull off my bathing suit.

Thank you for telling me!

4. The child care person tells Jake that trying to pull off someone's bathing suit or any other kind of clothes is not a safe game.

It is okay to play. It is **not** okay to pull off a bathing suit.

THE SLEEPOVER

Anytime you have a **problem**, your job is to **get help**, even if you have to wake up a grown-up in the middle of the night.

1. Simon likes to go to his cousin's house for a sleepover. They jump on the bed and laugh.

2. It gets dark and a little scary. They like cuddling together to feel safe.

3. Simon's cousin starts to crowd over to his side of the bed. Simon moves away so much that he falls out of bed.

4. Simon goes to get help from his aunt even though it is the middle of the night.

5. Simon's aunt just wants him to go back to bed. He **keeps telling her until she understands and helps him**.

"What are you doing up? Go back to bed."

"I can't sleep."

6. Simon's aunt makes a bed for him on the couch so he can be comfortable.

"Thanks, Auntie."

"Sleep well."

THE 'UH OH' FEELING

An 'Uh Oh' Feeling is your body telling you when something does not seem safe. When you feel **uncomfortable** about anything, always **get help from adults you trust**.

1. Sam enjoys going to his gym class.

2. His gym teacher Mr. Smith is fun and likes to take lots of photos of everyone.

3. When Mr. Smith wants to take photos of Sam by himself, Sam gets an 'uh oh' feeling.

"Put this shirt on for a special photo. This will be our secret."

"Photos should not be secrets. Stop or I'll tell."

4. Mr. Smith gets upset. Sam does not feel safe so he tells a Safety Lie and makes an Emergency Promise.

"Please don't tell!"

"I won't tell if you stop."

5. Even though Mr. Smith stops, Sam tells his father about the special photos, the Safety Lie, and the Emergency Promise.

"Thank you for telling. We will make sure this doesn't happen again."

6. Sam's father gets help.

KEEP TELLING UNTIL YOU GET HELP

Sometimes you have to be persistent and keep asking until you get the help you need. Remember that it is **never too late to tell**.

1. Kids at school locked Pearl in the bathroom. She was scared.

2. Pearl tells her dog. He listens but he cannot help her.

"Kids locked me in the bathroom. I was scared."

3. Pearl tells her Mom. She is too busy to understand.

"Kids locked me in the bathroom. I was scared."

"It's okay. Kids tease sometimes."

4. Pearl tells her Grandpa. He listens, but not for very long.

"Kids locked me in the bathroom. I was scared."

"That's not nice. I had a hard day too. My boss got mad at me!"

5. The Safety Rule is to tell a grown-up you trust when you have problems and to keep telling until someone helps.

"I will keep telling until someone helps me. Who else can I talk to next?"

6. Pearl's teacher listens. She understands and helps her.

"Kids locked me in the bathroom at school yesterday. I was scared."

"Oh my! Thank you for telling me. We will make sure you feel safe at school."

THE BUSY MOM

Adults cannot know what you are thinking, and they sometimes don't understand.
You might need to explain and say, "This is about my safety!"

THE TIRED GRANDPA
Even if your grown-ups are tired, grumpy, or busy, they care about your safety!

1. Sheri is sad because she is getting teased about her wheelchair.

2. She needs help, but her grandpa is asleep.

3. Sheri wakes her grandpa up, but he is tired.

4. Sheri persists because her feelings are hurt.

5. Her grandpa listens because Sheri's safety is important.

6. Her grandpa helps Sheri feel better, and they will make a Safety Plan to stop kids from teasing her.

'PEOPLE SAFETY' SKILLS TO STOP BULLYING

Use your awareness, move out of reach, protect your feelings, and speak up to take charge of your safety when kids try to hurt you, scare you, or make you feel bad.

1. If someone tries to bully you by being scary, you can use your **Walk Away Power and Get Help**. Being mean back will make the problem bigger, not better.

2. If someone tries to bully you by saying rude things, you can **throw the hurting words in your Trash Can**, and say something kind to yourself.

3. If someone tries to bully you by taking your turn, you can say, '**STOP! Please wait!**'

4. If someone tries to bully you by tripping or pushing, you can **use your awareness** to notice what this person is trying to do, and then **Move Out of Reach**.

MORE WAYS TO STOP BULLYING

You have the **right to be safe and respected** everywhere you go, and the responsibility to **act safely and respectfully** towards yourself and others.

1. If friends try to bully you by telling you not to play with someone else, **you do not have to do what they say.**

2. If someone tries to bully you by not letting you join the game, you can **keep asking**. If you see this happen to someone else, you can **speak up, or get help**.

3. If some kids try to bully you by leaving you out, you can **protect your feelings**, and **find someone else** to be your friend!

4. You have the **right to be safe** with your feelings and your body. If you need help to stop bullying problems, you can **ask the adults in charge for help**.

TATTLING AND TELLING — WHAT'S THE DIFFERENCE?

Tattling is when you are telling on kids just to get them into trouble.
Telling to get help is when you are asking for **help to solve a problem** with someone.

1. Don't tell on kids just because they are not doing what you think they should.

2. Unless there is a safety problem, **stay in charge of what you are doing** instead of what other kids are doing.

3. **Telling to get help is not tattling** or being a tattletale.

4. Sometimes grown-ups get confused about the difference between 'tattling' and 'telling to get help.'

5. You might need to **persist** in getting help.

6. Tell your grown-ups any time you have a **safety problem**.

© A publication of Kidpower Teenpower Fullpower International® www.kidpower.org For permission to copy, contact safety@kidpower.org

KYLE STAYS SAFE WITH HIS BODY

Feeling hurt or angry about being teased is normal. Instead of hitting or kicking someone when we are upset, we can **use our power to act safely, no matter how we feel inside.**

1. Kyle gets upset when a kid teases him. He wants to hit the kid to get even.

2. Kyle uses his power to act safely with his body, no matter how he feels inside. It is hard work, but Kyle uses his Hands Down Power to stop his body from hitting, and his Calm Down Power by taking a breath.

3. Instead of getting into a fight, Kyle uses his Mouth Closed Power and his Walk Away Power to leave and get away from the kid who is trying to bother him. If Kyle feels upset about what happened or if the girl keeps bothering him, Kyle will ask for help from an adult he trusts.

SAFETY WITH CARS
Use your awareness, stay together, and Check First!

NOT SAFE
Running into the street is **not safe**.

SAFE
Your safety rule is to **stop, look, and wait** for your grown-up.

NOT SAFE
Even if you are with a grown-up, it is **not safe** to walk in front of a car until it has stopped all the way.

SAFE
Your safety rule is to **look and wait** until the street is clear or until the cars all have stopped.

NOT SAFE
When a car backs up in a driveway, the driver cannot see a kid on a bike. It is **not safe** to go or ride your bike behind a car that is backing up.

SAFE
Wait until the car stops before you cross the driveway.

7. NOT SAFE
It is **not safe** to walk away from your grown-up when you get out of your car.

8. SAFE
Your safety rule is to **stay next to your grown-up** when you are outside your car.

THE BIG SISTER

Dedicated to the big sisters and big brothers everywhere who use their power to help keep their younger brothers and sisters safe!

1. Zara's little brother wants to go out the door. She holds the door closed.

2. Zara's little brother tries to climb out the window. She grabs him and yells for help.

3. Zara's little brother tries to get out of his car seat while they are driving. Zara yells for help.

4. Zara's little brother tries to climb over the wall and into the water with the ducks. Zara grabs him and yells for help. Her little brother is annoyed. Her parents thank her for stopping him from falling into the pond, while still staying safe herself.

kidpower Safety Signals for Everyone, Everywhere To Help Prevent And Solve Problems

Safety Signals are simple gestures, drawings, and words to help all of us remember important 'People Safety' ideas and skills.

Wait Power

Hold your own hands as a reminder of when you need to wait patiently to stay safe and be respectful.

Stay Aware Power

Point towards your eyes, turn your head, and look around as a reminder of how to pay attention and act alert.

Stay Together Power

Start with your palms apart and facing outwards, and then move them together as a reminder to stay together to stay safe out in public.

Check First Power

Gently clasp your own forearm as a reminder to get permission from your adults or to let people who care about you know before you change your plan about where you are doing, who is with you, or what you are doing.

Think First Power

Pat your head gently as a reminder to Think First about what to do when the unexpected happens or when someone is acting unsafely.

Walk Away Power

Walk in place with your feet as a reminder to walk away from trouble and get to Safety.

Roll Away Power

Roll your fingers along your arm as a reminder to use wheels to roll away from trouble and get to Safety.

Get Help Power

Put your arms in front of you with palms facing up as a reminder to reach out to others to get help or to make a connection.

© A publication of Kidpower Teenpower Fullpower International® www.kidpower.org For permission to copy, contact safety@kidpower.org

kidpower Safety Signals For Taking Charge Of Our Feelings, Words, And Bodies

The keys to remembering to use 'People Safety' strategies and skills in real life are simplicity, repetition, consistency, fun, and practice.

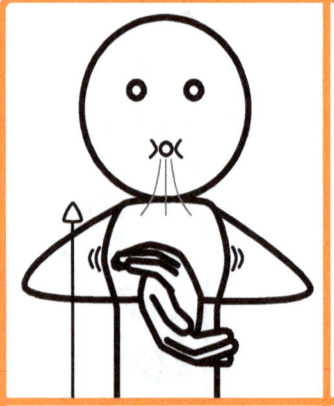  

Calm Down Power

Press your palms together, straighten your back, breathe deeply and slowly, and feel your feet on the ground to help yourself calm down if you are scared or angry.

Mouth Closed Power

Squeeze your lips together as a reminder that you can stop yourself from saying or doing anything unsafe with your mouth.

Hands And Feet Down Power

Put your arms down to your sides and your feet firmly on the ground as a reminder to stop yourself from bothering or hurting someone with your hands or feet.

Hang On Power

Hang onto your sides or pockets to stop yourself from touching or hitting someone.

Speak Up Power

Put your hand in front of your mouth and move it outwards as a reminder to speak up about what you do and do not want.

Fence Power

Put your arms in front of yourself waist-high with palms facing downwards as a reminder to make a fence and set boundaries with someone who is bothering you.

Trash Can Power

Put a hand on your hip and pretend the hole it makes is your personal trash can. Use your other hand to catch hurtful words and throw them away as a reminder to protect yourself from hurtful messages instead of taking them inside.

Heart Power

Reach forward and then press your hands onto your chest as a reminder to take kindness into your heart. Hold your hands on your chest to protect your heart and to use your heart to be kind to others.

kidpower Safety Signals For Building Better Relationships

We can have more fun and fewer problems with people when we use these Safety Powers.

Listening Power

Put one hand behind your ear as a reminder that listening to others helps you learn and understand.

Speak Up Power

Put your hand in front of your mouth and move it outwards as a reminder to speak up about what you do and do not want.

No, Thank You Power

Put your hand up, palm out, and shake your head as a reminder that even if you really like someone, you can say, "No, thank you!" to anything that makes you or others less safe.

Teamwork Power

Clasp your fingers together in front of you as a reminder that, when we cooperate with each other, things work better for everyone.

Appreciation Power (Hooray Power!)

Shake your hands in the air or clap your hands with enthusiasm as a reminder that when we cheer for people, we are letting them know that we appreciate them.

Make A Bridge Power

Put your hands in front of you waist-high with palms facing up as a reminder to connect with someone to get help, join an activity, or just talk.

Make A Fence Power

Put your hands in front of you waist high with palms facing down as a reminder that you can set a boundary to let someone know that you want them to stop behavior that you don't like.

Make A Wall Power

Put your hands in front of your chest with palms facing out as a reminder to protect yourself when someone is acting unsafely by making a clear barrier between yourself and that person.

kidpower Safety Signal For Taking Charge Of Our Safety

If someone is acting in a way that feels unsafe, we can make safer choices using these Safety Powers

Stay Aware Power

Point towards your eyes, turn your head, and look around as a reminder to pay attention and stay alert.

Voice Power

Use a loud and powerful voice to get attention and help in an emergency or to stop someone who is acting unsafely.

Look Away Power

Look away instead of staring if someone gets uncomfortable or needs privacy. Look away and get help if you see something unsafe online or in person.

Stop Power

Make your hands like a wall and say, "Stop!" as a reminder of what you can do if someone tries to bother you.

Walk Away Power (Alternative version)

Walk your fingers like two little legs along your arm as a reminder to walk away from trouble and get to safety.

Roll Away Power

Roll your fingers along your arm as a reminder to use wheels to roll away from trouble and get to safety.

Get Help Power (Find Safety)

Put your hands out in front of you with your palms facing up as a reminder to go to Safety and reach out to someone in order to Get Help.

Persistence Power

Put your hands a few inches apart facing each other about shoulder high. Move them back and forth as a reminder to be persistent, keep going, and not give up when you need help or are setting a boundary.

kidpower Safety Signals For Healthy Boundaries With People We Know

These Safety Signals help everyone, everywhere remember the boundary rules and principles for staying safe and having fun with people we know.

Safety Signals for The Four Kidpower Boundary Rules

We each belong to ourselves
Point to yourself, sit tall, and smile as a reminder that each person's body, time, feelings, and thoughts are important.

Some things are not a choice
Shrug and smile as a reminder that some things are required, even for adults.

Problems should not be secrets
Hold a finger in front of your mouth. Move the finger away from your mouth as a reminder that we are safer when we can talk about our problems.

Keep telling until you get help
Have one hand say, 'I need help.' and the other hand reply, 'I will help you.' as a reminder to tell until you get help.

Safety Signals for the Kidpower Consent Checklist: Touch, attention, and games for play, affection, and fun, should be safe, the choice of each person, allowed by the adults in charge, and not a secret, which means others can know.

Safe
Hug yourself as a reminder that we all deserve to be and feel safe.

The choice of each person
Put two thumbs up as a reminder that each person needs to agree about touch, attention, and games for play, affection, and fun.

Allowed by the adults in charge
Curl your hand up and pretend it is the head of an adult in charge nodding in approval as a reminder that the adults in charge need to agree it is allowed.

Not a secret, so others can know
Open your hands and raise both arms above your head as a reminder that touch, play, and affection should not be a secret.

© A publication of Kidpower Teenpower Fullpower International® www.kidpower.org For permission to copy, contact safety@kidpower.org

BEST FRIENDS AND MISTAKES
A Kidpower Teaching Story

NOTE: This is an interactive story, which can be read to one child or to a group of kids. Encourage each child to respond to the questions by nodding or shaking their head, raising their hand, or answering out loud. Adapt the directions depending on the child or children with you. Change names if necessary so that no child you are reading to has the same names as the children in the story.

Even though you know lots of ways to stay safe, it can be hard to remember what to do in real life. Once a girl who learned Kidpower went to her best friend's house for an overnight. We do not use the real names of our students, so we will call her Penny, and her friend, Kerry. [Change the names if the child you are reading to has that same name.]

Have any of you stayed overnight at a friend's house? [Encourage children to respond.] Penny and Kerry decided to stay awake after Kerry's parents told them to go to sleep. Have any of you ever stayed up after adults told you to go to sleep? [Encourage children to respond.]

After everybody was asleep, Kerry said to Penny, "I'm hungry! Let's go sneak some chips from the kitchen!" Have any of you ever snuck treats when you weren't supposed to? [Encourage children to respond.] Then Kerry said, "Let's go watch something on the computer. I just found a movie for grownups that I know we're not supposed to see. OK?"

Penny thought this sounded exciting and said, "OK!" even though she knew it was against the rules. She felt like grownups make too many rules! Do any of you ever feel like there are **too many rules**? [Encourage children to respond.] Have any of you ever broken rules on purpose? [Encourage children to respond.]

Anyway, while they were snuggled together eating chips and watching the movie, Penny started to feel uncomfortable about what she was seeing. She thought, "This is gross. But I don't want Kerry to think I'm a baby! And what do adults know anyway!" So she said nothing. Have any of you ever not wanted your friends to think you were a baby? [Encourage children to respond.]

Suddenly, Kerry started touching Penny between her legs in her private area. Penny was shocked. She thought, "This is my best friend. I don't want her to get mad at me. But I'm starting to feel real bad! And I already broke a lot of rules. Being up late, sneaking the chips, watching the movie. I can't stop now. And who could I talk to? I don't know Kerry's parents that well. They might get mad at me."

Penny was so confused that she just waited and did nothing. What other choices did Penny have? [Let the children answer. If they get stuck, prompt them.] Could she tell Kerry to stop? Would Kerry be a good friend to get mad at Penny if she says to stop? If you make one mistake, should you keep on making mistakes? Could Penny call home? Even in the middle of the night? Check with your parents so that you know that you can always call if you have a problem, even in the middle of the night.

Penny felt so upset about what happened that she pushed it out of her mind. It took a lot of work, but every time the memory came up, she made herself forget. Have you ever made yourself forget things you felt bad about? [Encourage children to respond.]

About a week later, Penny had a bad dream. She woke up and said to herself, "Oh, no, that wasn't just a dream. It really happened! I broke all my safety rules. I feel like such a bad person. And I feel so mixed up about Kerry. She did something that makes me feel bad, but she's my best friend. It's been a whole week! I can't tell anybody about it now!" What other choices does Penny have? [Wait for suggestions] Is it **ever** too late to ask for help? No, it is **never** too late to tell.

Penny kept feeling bad and making herself forget for a whole year. Then she tried to tell her mother. [Or father] She said, "Mom, Kerry is acting funny."

Her Mom said, "What do you mean by funny?"

Penny said, "Well, she makes me uncomfortable."

Penny's mom said, "That's okay, honey. Things do change with friends, as you get older. Why don't you try talking with Kerry or play with someone else?"

Penny went away feeling really upset, though she did not show her mother. She thought, "Mom does not care about what happened to me! I've felt so awful for so long and she doesn't even care!" What do you think? Does Penny's Mom care about her? [Wait for response] What else could Penny have done? [Wait for suggestions and coach answers.] Did she tell her Mom the whole story? Can her Mom read her mind?

Finally, Penny tried to tell her Mom again. She said, "Mom, something has really bothered me for a long time, and I'm scared you'll get mad that I didn't tell you sooner. But one time I was at Kerry's house and we stayed up and watched a movie that we weren't supposed to, and she touched me in a way that I know broke our safety rules about touching private areas. And I feel like a really bad person."

Penny's Mom said, "You're not bad, Penny, you just made a mistake. And I'm glad you told me now. We'll talk some more until you feel better. And we'll talk to Kerry's family. I'm sure she needs help too."

Penny, Kerry, and their grownups all got the help they needed to be safe and to feel good about themselves.

Sometimes the people kids love have problems. Sometimes their problems are so big that they do things to hurt kids or make them uncomfortable. If this happens to you or to someone you know, it does not mean that anybody is bad. But it does mean that everyone needs help. The way to get help is to tell an adult you trust. If the first adult you tell does not understand, try again. If this adult does not help, find another adult to tell. If an adult tells you not to talk about it, tell a different adult. Keep telling until somebody does something about the problem. Remember that what happened is **not** your fault, and that it is **never** too late to tell.

Discussions And Practices To Build Understanding And Skills

How To Make Discussing, Practicing, And Using These Skills Successful

The more that everyone in a family, school, or youth group has a common understanding about safety, the safer they are. For this reason, we recommend that you read the stories together, act out what the people are doing in the drawings, and discuss how these ideas might work in your daily lives.

We will be safer and have better relationships if we keep using these skills in everyday life. Coach kids to be successful in avoiding and solving problems with people—in the same way that you might prepare them to be safe with water, food, fire, cars, and bikes—at home, in your neighborhood, in nature, at school, at work, and in your community

Don't let discomfort get in the way of safety. Review the Safety Plans and the 'People Safety' skills in this book with children on a regular basis. Give special attention to actions that might be hard due to embarrassment, such as interrupting busy adults when you have a problem, yelling to get help, or speaking up if someone is bullying. Although feeling embarrassed, upset, or shy is normal, not letting uncomfortable emotions stop us from getting help or making the safest choices is important.

Stay relevant by adapting these examples and practices to make sense for each person's age, life situation, and abilities. Tell younger children or kids who think very literally, "I am just pretending so we can practice!" If necessary, simplify the information by using fewer words, or change the wording to ensure understanding. You can also expand on the concepts presented by discussing with young people how to adapt these skills and ideas to handle more complicated situations.

Instead of testing or tricking children, coach them to be successful. When you are practicing, pause to give kids a chance to try to use the skill. If they get stuck, coach them in exactly what to say, how to say it, and what to do with their bodies, as if you were the director or a prompter in a play. Encourage children to project an assertive attitude of both power and respect in their body language, choice of words, and posture, rather than acting either passively or aggressively.

Make the practices fun by being positive and calm rather than anxious. Reward small steps with encouragement, remembering that mistakes are part of learning. Celebrate progress rather than looking for perfection.

Keep the focus on how to stay safe rather than on the bad things that can happen. Going into detail about the ways we can get hurt just makes kids anxious without making them safer. Worrying and talking about safety problems can feel as if we are doing something—and are not nearly as effective as actually having a clear plan and practicing how to implement it so that we are prepared to take action.

Give discussing, practicing, and using these skills the same priority that you give other issues related to health and safety. These are crucial skills that can prevent problems and improve relationships. If you encounter resistance, you can acknowledge that it is normal to not want to practice and to feel as if we already know what to do. However, rehearsing how to handle different kinds of problems is for our safety and must be a high priority. Discussing is not the same as actually practicing. Even if they express lots of resistance, most children also enjoy showing that they know what to do.

Directions For Discussion And Practices

Page 9 — Kidpower Protection Promise

Discuss this message often with all children in your life, making it relevant for their situations. Remind yourself to be a safe person for kids to come to by really listening with calm compassion even if a concern does not seem important to you or seems like the child's fault, without lecturing, scolding, or joking.

Page 10 — Be and act aware, calm, respectful, and confident

Explain that "People bother you less and listen to you more if you act aware, calm, respectful, and confident." Discuss what these words mean.

To practice, coach children to stand or sit tall and turn their heads to look around. Walk behind them and do something silly for them to look at. Ask them to tell you what they saw so you know they are really looking around. Next, let children start close to you and walk towards another spot a little ways from you, glancing back to see what you are doing and then looking where they are going. Again, do something silly for them to report when they get to their spot.

Pages 11-13 — Use different kinds of power and move away from trouble

We want children to know that there are many ways to be powerful. Coach children to squeeze their lips together to use Mouth Closed Power. Coach children to raise their hands as they are about to hit or touch something they shouldn't and instead pull their hands down to their sides to use Hands Down Power. Coach children to put their hands in front of themselves like a wall and say, "Stop!" to use Stop Power.

Pretend to be another kid who is starting to get mad, or who is about to throw things or shove on the playground or in line. Coach children to use their Walk Away Power to move out of reach. With an individual child, you can come up with even more ideas of different ways to be powerful.

Use the coaching guide on the bottom of page 12 to practice *Moving Out Of Reach*. Start close together and have kids practice backing away. You can then act out the *Leaving Story* and the *Walk Away Power Story* by pretending to be a grumpy kid and having kids practice moving away from you with awareness, calm, and respectful confidence.

Pages 14-17 — Stay Together, Check First, and know how to Get Help everywhere you go

Unless children are independent enough to be somewhere or do something without an adult supervising their safety, their best self-protection strategy is almost always to Check First with their adults before they change their plan about what they are doing, who is with them, and where they are going - including with people they know.

Practice the Check First rule using relevant examples from a child's life, such as: before you open the door, before you use the stove, before you get close to an animal at the park (you can use a toy animal to pretend), before you pick up something sharp, before going with a friendly neighbor even if this is a kid who invites you to do something fun, and before you get close to someone you don't know well. Coach children to stand up, move away, and go to their adults to Check First. Say, "Your Mom says you are supposed to come to my house." Coach kids to walk away as they say, "I need to Check First myself!"

| Pages 18-22 | Know how to be safe with strangers |

During your daily life, point out people who are strangers and people who children know well. Discuss that a stranger can know your name or wear a uniform. Remind kids that most people are good, and that most strangers are good. However, if you don't know someone well, you Check First before you get close to, talk with, or take anything from someone you don't know well.

To practice, pretend to be a stranger. Approach the child calling the child's name or holding something that belongs to the child. Coach the child to stand up, move away, and go to his or her adult to Check First. You can have another adult or child or even a toy pretending to be this child's grown-up. Have this person say, "Thank you for Checking First!"

While you are pretending to be the "stranger," act like someone who just doesn't know the safety rules rather than being scary. Coach kids to be successful in standing up and moving away rather than you getting too close to them. Reinforce their understanding of keeping a distance from people the child doesn't know well by staying far away from them when you are practicing Stranger Safety skills.

| Pages 23-24 | Know your Safety Plan if you are having an emergency |

Children need to know the exceptions to the Check First rules. Make and review your family's Safety Plan for getting help each time your child goes to a new place. Pretend you are about to go into a store or park, and coach children to ask, "What's our safety plan if we get lost?" A plan that uses a mobile phone should also have a backup plan in case it doesn't work.

Encourage children to buy something from the cashier so that they know how to interact with this person. Take children to the place you want them to go if they are lost or bothered in a store or out in public. Make sure they can find this place if they need help. If children cannot follow their Safety Plan, discuss backup plans for getting help that make sense for that situation, such as asking for help from a woman with children, calling police, etc. Unless they are having a big emergency, children should not leave the place you were planning for them to be.

Tell children, "The rules are different in emergencies. You might need to get help from people you don't know if you are hurt, someone is making you feel scared, or you are lost in nature. You might need to go to a safer place to get away from a fire or other big safety emergency."

Getting help in public can be embarrassing. Pretend to be a busy, impatient cashier, and coach children to come to the front of the line, interrupt you, and be persistent in asking for help because they are being bothered by someone, their friend is hurt, or they are lost.

Practice with children yelling for help as if they have hurt their leg and can't move. If they are lost outdoors where there are no stores, coach them to stay where they are if it is safe to do so and to call for help, and to accept help from a ranger or other stranger such as a woman with children or a person calling their name.

| Page 25 | Know when to wait and when to interrupt |

Explain to children that they might need to wait when they want something – and, if there is a Safety Problem, their job is to interrupt their adult and to keep asking until they get help. Pretend to be busy, busy, busy. Tell children to imagine that there is a Safety Problem such as a kid bothering another kid or being about to run into the street. Coach them to interrupt you and to tell you what the problem is.

Act irritated when they interrupt you and coach them to say, "This is about Safety." to get your attention. End by saying, "Thank you for interrupting me."

Page 26	Yell, leave, and get help if you are scared

Pretend to be someone acting a little unsafely (not in a frightening way). Say something like, "Hey kid, get over here!" Avoid speaking or acting in ways that might put scary or upsetting images into a child's mind. Do not pretend to grab a child.

Remember success-based learning—coach kids to set a firm boundary and to use a strong yelling voice. Coach children to put their hands in front of their chests with their arms slightly bent and palms facing out to make a wall and yell, "STOP!" As the pretend Scary Person, act startled and stop. Coach children to run to Safety, yelling "I NEED HELP!" Coach someone pretending to be their adult to say, "I will help you."

Page 27	The Arm Grab Escape

Practice the arm grab escape with children one at a time by grabbing one of their arms gently but firmly. When practicing, you are holding your child's arms hard enough so they feel a little trapped, but not so hard that you bruise them, injure them, or make it impossible for them to escape. The goal is for them to learn the technique.

Have the child standing up in front of you and grab their arm making sure there is enough room around you so they do not bump into things when practicing. Keep in mind that the child will be pulling away from you so they need more space behind them. Coach them to clasp their hands together (make sure they are not intertwining their fingers) and use the leverage of their arm by turning and moving their body away and keeping their arm close to their body. When practicing, they should yell loudly, "NO" when they pull away—and then also practice going to Safety.

The first time you practice, let go as soon as you feel the child pull away. Kids can pull away with a lot of force so be prepared and make sure they are also in balance and prepared to catch themselves when they pull away. Then let the child practice again and hold on a little tighter. Coach children to pull their hands out against the place where your fingertips come together with your thumb, because this spot is the weakest part of someone's grip. Coach them to yell, "NO!" and "HELP!" loudly while pulling away.

Page 28	Introduce boundaries

Teach the 4 Kidpower Boundary Rules on page 28 to your children and find examples to show what these rules look like in their daily lives. Use *The Bath Story* to help kids see how the rules fit together.

Pages 30-35	Protect your feelings from hurting words and taking in compliments

Children are emotionally safest if they can take in the kind things people say to them or they say to themselves and protect themselves from hurtful messages. To practice, coach children to pretend to catch hurting words in the air, throw them into a real trash can or a trash can they make with their bodies, and say something nice to themselves.

Put a hand on your hip and show that the hole makes a personal Trash Can. Practice together—for example, if someone says, "You are stupid," children can catch the word "STUPID," throw it in their personal Trash Can and say, "I am SMART!"

Make sure children know that you are just pretending so they can practice and that you do not mean the words you are saying. Do not have children practice saying hurtful words to each other — you want them to focus on the skills for protecting their feelings.

Give children meaningful compliments for them to take into their hearts while saying, "Thank you!" Have them practice giving compliments to each other— and to you!

Discuss how they can use the Kidpower Trash Can Technique to protect their feelings from their own Negative Self-Talk – the unkind things that they say to themselves – and how they can use Positive Self-Talk by taking in compliments and giving themselves kind messages.

Page 36	Teach children the safety rules about consent

The Kidpower Consent Checklist is: Touch, attention, or games for play, affection, or fun should be okay with each person, safe, allowed by the adults in charge, and not a secret so others can know.

Play the "Asking for a hug" game by having children ask you, "May I have a hug?" Say, "No, thanks. No hugs today. We can wave instead." And wave. Then reverse roles and ask, "May I have a hug?" Coach children to say, "No, thanks. No hugs today. Just wave." And wave. This practice lets children rehearse setting and accepting boundaries on unwanted touch for affection.

Practice saying yes or no to touch and games by having kids take turns saying, "Let's _____, (play tag, wrestle, have a race, or play catch)!" Coach them both to give and respect different responses. For example, "That's great!" Or, "No, thanks!" Or, "We'll have to go outside because we might break things inside." Or, "Not in the street!" Or, "Not at the dinner table!"

Pages 37-39	Understanding about choice

The second Kidpower Boundary Rule is "Some things are not a choice" - and "Allowed by the adults in charge" is part of the Consent Checklist. Use the examples to discuss what is and is not a choice for children – and encourage them to come up with their own examples.

Discuss these stories and examples to help children to understand what is and is not their choice, when they can set boundaries, how to respect the choices of others, and that it should be okay to tell your adults about any kind of touch.

Page 40	Stop unwanted touch or teasing

The skills shown in the story *How to Stop Unwanted Touch* prepare children to persist in setting boundaries if someone doesn't notice, doesn't listen, tries to make them feel wrong by using emotional coercion, offers a bribe, or makes them promise not to tell. Teach children to use their voices, bodies, and words to set clear boundaries with people they know, such as family, friends, and peers.

To practice, put a hand on a child's shoulder and say, "Suppose you like my hand on your shoulder. If you like this touch, it is fine. But can you change your mind? Yes, you can. Now, pretend you don't like this touch any more." Coach children to give you back your hand in a firm, polite way and say, in a clear, respectful voice, "Please stop." Pretend not to listen; put your hand back. Coach children to stand or move back, make a fence with their hands, look at you and say in a calm, firm voice, and say in a powerful and respectful way, "I said, 'Please stop!' I don't like it."

Next, pretend to be sad or annoyed so children can practice dealing with emotional coercion. Say, "But I like you. I thought you were my friend." Coach children to project an assertive attitude by being both firm and polite while they say, "I don't mean to hurt your feelings. I am your friend, and I still want you to stop." Or just, "Sorry and stop!"

Discuss when bribes are safe or unsafe. Practice resisting unsafe bribes. Say, "I'll give you a treat (offer something you think the child you are practicing with would like) if you let me touch your shoulder after you asked me to stop. But don't tell anybody, okay?" Coach each child to say, "Stop or I'll tell!" You can coach them to add, "I don't keep touch or gifts a secret."

For children who can understand (normally children over 5 or 6 years old), give them the chance to practice promising not to tell even though they are going to tell an adult they trust as soon as they can. Pretend to get angry or upset without acting intensely or making specific threats. Say, "Promise not to tell anyone or something bad will happen!" Or, "You have to promise not to tell or I won't be able to play with you anymore." Or, "Please don't tell, or I could get into trouble."

Coach children to say, "I won't tell if you stop." Explain that, "Most of the time we want you to tell the truth and keep your promises. But you can lie and break a promise to stay safe, as long as you get away as soon as you can and tell an adult you trust and keep telling until someone does something about it."

Page 41	Know the difference between safe and unsafe secrets
	Very young children should just be taught not to keep anything a secret. As they get older, discuss the difference between a surprise party or gift that everyone knows about except the person being surprised (who will find out) and a secret that breaks your safety rules that most people will NOT know about.
Page 42	Know the difference between safe and unsafe bribes
	Discuss the difference between rewards that you get for doing something helpful or good for you and bribes to get you to do something against your safety rules and that might hurt you or someone else.
Pages 43-46	Kidpower safety rules about private areas
	Discuss your family's rules about private areas with your child in a calm and matter-of-fact way. Make sure to review your safety rules about private areas about every six months. The Kidpower Safety Rule is: "Your Private areas are the parts of your body that can be covered by a two-piece bathing suit. For play or teasing, other people should not try to touch your private areas, nor should they try to get you to touch their private areas. For health or safety, your grownups might need to touch your private areas and it should never have to be a secret. People should not show kids pictures or videos about people and their private areas – and they should not try to take pictures or videos about their private areas. Anything about private areas should not have to be a secret. Even if the person stops, you can always tell an adult you trust."
Page 47	Keep kids safe from inappropriate or upsetting online material
	Children need adult protection from seeing or hearing about inappropriate or upsetting material online - or anywhere else. Remember that even if they are right next to you, if you are not looking at the same screen as your child, they may access unsafe material online. Have clear safety rules about Checking First with you before they explore online and before they contact anyone or share personal information online.

It is normal for kids to be curious and they might accidentally or intentionally click on a link, video, or picture that leads to emotionally unsafe content. It is important that adults do not shame children for being curious or interested in concepts that aren't openly or routinely discussed. They need to know clearly from their adults that their curiosity is normal and positive. The problem is that so much of what is found online is misinformation and we need to make sure they are getting accurate information about sensitive topics.

Discuss *The Curiosity Story* to acknowledge their interest and to encourage kids to tell you if they have any questions or see anything inappropriate or upsetting online or anywhere else. Also, consider providing them with books that help answer questions they may be too embarrassed to ask you about.

Even with the best supervision at home, children may see inappropriate content in a friend or family member's home or hear about it in graphic detail from another child.

Reinforce the Kidpower safety rules so that your child has a plan if this should happen and remind them that you will help them.

Tell kids, "Sometimes the things we see online are untrue or unsafe. Anything you do, see, or hear about should not have to be a secret from your adults. Please tell me if you see or hear about anything online that makes you feel uncomfortable including if it is about people and their private areas or people hurting each other. I will answer any questions that you have."

Pages 48-50   Go and get help when you have a problem and keep telling until you get help

Remind children that touch, games, presents, money, activities, photos, videos, and problems should not be secrets. Discuss different safety problems children might have and who to ask for help if they need it. Tell children to pretend to have a safety problem. Pretend to be a busy adult (act as if you are reading a book, watching TV, or working). Coach children to interrupt you to ask for help. Say, "I'm busy."

Coach children to ask again. Say, "Don't bother me." Coach children to say, "This is about my safety." Listen, coaching children to tell the whole story. Say, "Thank you for telling me." If children do this well, do the practice again. This time be unsupportive by saying, "That's your problem. Go away." Coach children to persist and to think of other adults they might go to for help.

Remind children of the Kidpower Protection Promise on page 9. Tell them, "Sometimes the people who are important to kids or to their families have problems, and sometimes their problems are so big that they do things to hurt kids or to make them uncomfortable. If this happens to you or someone else, it is not your fault even if you made a mistake. And it does NOT mean that anyone is bad. It just means that everyone needs help. Find adults you trust and tell and keep telling until you get the help you need. If one adult doesn't listen or understand, then find another adult to tell. Remember that it is NEVER too late to tell."

Pages 51-52   Know what bullying is and how to stop it

Point out examples of bullying as they happen in real life, in stories, or in movies such as shunning, name-calling, intimidation, etc. Pretend to act like someone who is bullying by saying something mean. Coach the child to use their Trash Can and move away or coach the child to say, "Stop." - and then to leave to get help.

Coach kids in how to ask confidently and positively to be included. Discuss how to persist if they are excluded at first. Start by coaching the child to say, "I want to play." Or, "I want to join you." Pretend to reject the child by frowning and saying,

"Go away. You're not good enough." Or, "There's too many already." Have the child throw away the hurting words and say to themselves, "I'm great." Coach the child to practice persisting instead of getting upset or giving up by saying in a cheerful and confident way, "I'll do my best." Or, "I'll get better if I practice." Or, "There's always room for one more." Or, "Give me a chance." Or, "The rule at school is everybody gets to play." Coach a child who is being left out to go find another child and invite that child to play - and to ask for help from an adult.

Give a more verbal child the chance to practice being an advocate. Pretend to be unkind to someone else. Coach the child to say, "Stop. That is not kind!" Pretend to exclude another person so that the child can practice speaking up for someone else by saying, "Let her play!" Or, "Give them a chance!"

Pretend to be another child who is acting unsafely. Push the child gently and say something like, "Get over here, you dummy!" Coach the child to take a breath, throw the mean words away, use Mouth Closed Power by not answering back, and Walk Away Power by standing tall and leaving with awareness. Remind the child to go to an adult and get help because problems should not be secrets.

Discuss the *Kyle Stays Safe With His Body* story to remind kids that they can stay in charge of what they say and do even if someone else is being unkind.

Page 53	Know the difference between tattling and telling to get help
	Too often, kids don't talk about safety problems because they have been told not to "tattle" or be a "tattletale." Try not to use these labels. Instead, encourage kids to focus on their own responsibilities unless another kid is doing something that is unsafe—and to always talk about safety problems, even if someone will be annoyed with them.
Page 55	Safety with cars
	We added this page because families and schools asked us to show how Kidpower skills like Stay Aware, Stay Together, Wait, and Check First could also apply to being safe around cars.
Pages 57-61	Kidpower Safety Signals
	You can use these simple gestures, words, and drawings to review and help kids and adults remember core 'People Safety' strategies, safety rules, and skills. Visit the Kidpower.org website for posters or letter-size sets.
Pages 62-63	Best Friends and Mistakes Kidpower Teaching Story
	Best Friends and Mistakes is an interactive teaching story that helps children to integrate information about boundaries on touch and games and helps to prepare them in case they forget like Penny, the girl in the story, did. This also reminds kids that it is never too late to get help.

Kidpower Services For All Ages And Abilities

Kidpower Teenpower Fullpower International is a global nonprofit leader dedicated to providing effective and empowering child protection, positive communication, and personal safety skills for all ages and abilities. Since 1989, Kidpower has served millions of children, teenagers, and adults, including those with difficult life challenges, locally and around the world through our workshops, educational resources, and partnerships. We give our students the opportunity for successful practice of 'People Safety' skills in ways that helps prepare them to develop healthy relationships, increase their confidence, take charge of their emotional and physical safety, and act safely and respectfully towards others. For more information, visit **Kidpower.org** or contact safety@kidpower.org.

Workshops
Through both online and in-person services, Kidpower has led workshops in over 60 countries spanning six continents. Our programs include: Parent/Caregiver seminars; Parent-Child workshops; training for educators and other professionals; classroom workshops; Family workshops; Teenpower self-defense workshops for teens; Collegepower for young people leaving home; Fullpower self-defense and boundary-setting workshops for adults; Seniorpower for older people; adapted programs for people with special needs; and workplace safety, communication, and team-building seminars. Our Child Protection Advocates Training Program prepares educators and other professionals, as well as parents and other caring adults, to use Kidpower's intervention, advocacy, and personal safety skills in their personal and professional lives.

Kidpower Online Learning Center
Online training programs include: Professional Development and Facilitator Training Institute for teaching safety skills to people of all ages, abilities and walks of life; Kidpower for EVERY School Classroom Lessons; Bridges to People Safety for individuals with disabilities; and more.

Educational Resources Library
Our extensive online Library provides over 400 free 'People Safety' resources including articles, videos, webinars, blogs, and podcasts. Free downloads of online publications like our Kidpower Safety Signals, coloring book, and handouts are available for individual use. We provide licensing for use of materials or content for charitable and educational purposes.

Coaching, Consulting, and Curriculum Development
Long-distance coaching by video-conferencing, telephone, and e-mail enables us to make our services accessible worldwide. We consult with a wide range of experts, organizations, and schools on how best to adapt our program to meet unserved needs and develop new curriculum to increase the 'People Safety' knowledge for different people facing difficult life challenges.

Instructor Training and Center Development
Our very comprehensive certified instructor training program prepares qualified people to teach our programs under our auspices and to establish centers and offices for organizing services in their communities under our organizational umbrella.

Recommended Kidpower Curriculum Books

For Teaching 'People Safety' To Children and Youth From 3 to 14

Kidpower Confident Kids Safety Lessons and Assignments

The *Kidpower Confident Kids Safety Lessons* book provides 15 'People Safety' Lessons with cartoon illustrations and directions for short, up-beat, and fun practices. They prepare adult leaders to teach young people ages 6 to 14 to take charge of their emotional and physical safety with peers, acquaintances, and strangers and include Kidpower Positive Peer lessons for preventing and stopping bullying. The *Kidpower Confident Kids 10 Assignments* book provides pages that can be copied for a classroom, youth group, or family. These assignments make it easy to share key skills and safety rules from the *Kidpower Confident Kids Safety Lessons* with parents.

Kidpower Starting Strong

The *Starting Strong* curriculum is designed to make it fun and easy for educators to teach 'People Safety' lessons to groups of young children from about 3 to 7 years old.

The *Safety Lessons* book includes clear explanations, relevant social stories, and directions for practicing each set of skills along with adaptations for learning differences.

As a companion book, the *Teacher's Guide* provides crafts, games, suggestions for using the Kidpower skills to address different issues, take-home lessons for families, and adaptations for children with learning differences. The purpose is to build on the skills and knowledge taught in the Lessons book in order to help children develop strong safety habits that can stay with them throughout their lives.

The activities in these books are designed to be fun because children and adults alike learn better when they are having fun. Instead of dwelling on the bad things that might happen, Kidpower focuses on practicing what we can do to stay safe, which reduces worry and increases competence and confidence.

Kidpower Teaching Book Series

Each of the books in this series can stand on its own, or used in combination with the other Teaching Books. **Each book contains many more cartoon-illustrated lessons** from Kidpower's exceptional curriculum with additional explanations, stories, skill practice coaching guides of social-emotional skills that can help develop strong relationships, prevent most bullying, harassment, abuse, kidnapping, and other violence in ways that are age-appropriate, upbeat, emotionally safe, inclusive of kids with disabilities – and not scary.

Kidpower and Fullpower Social Stories

The *Social Stories* book series are designed to introduce or review skills through entertaining stories with clear hands-on group practices in each one to make them interactive while developing skills. Each book set targets 12 different safety skill-sets with a book sets for young children, youth, and teens and adults.

Online Kidpower Resources

Kidpower Downloadable Posters And Coloring Book

Kidpower Consent and Boundaries Posters (3 languages):
kidpower.org/library/consent-posters/

Posters of all the Kidpower Signals
kidpower.org/library/kidpower-safety-signals/

Kidpower Protection Promise Posters (3 languages):
kidpower.org/library/kidpower-protection-promise

Coloring Book for Young Children (11 languages):
kidpower.org/library/kidpower-coloring-book/

Kidpower Confident Kids Essential Safety Skills Posters:
kidpower.org/library/confident-kids/

Online Learning Center
learn.kidpower.org

Learn how to use and teach social-emotional safety skills that prepare people of all ages, abilities, and walks of life to prevent harm and strengthen relationships.

Courses provide videos, workbooks, and practice guides as well as opportunities for live coaching sessions.

Safety Powers for Teaching People With Communication Disabilities

Starting Strong for Teaching Children Ages 3-7

Teenpower Safety and Independence

Kidpower 30-Skills Coaching Handbook: Introductory Guide to Teaching Social-Emotional Safety Skills to Young People

Kidpower Online Resource Pages

Kidpower Social-Emotional Learning School Resources:
kidpower.org/schools/

Bullying Solutions Resources:
kidpower.org/bullying/

Protect Young People From Sexual Abuse:
kidpower.org/child-abuse-prevention/

Kidpower Resources For People Facing Prejudice:
kidpower.org/prejudice/

Resources For People With Special Needs:
www.kidpower.org/all-abilities/

Resources including books and articles in Spanish:
kidpower.org/espanol/

Additional Kidpower Books from Preschool Years to College Years

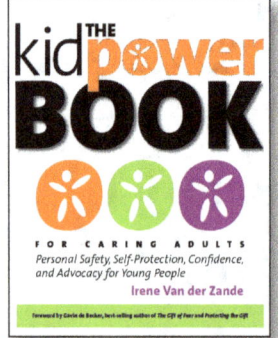

Acknowledgments

Thank you to each of the remarkable people from around the world for your gifts of commitment, creativity, time, talent, and generosity!

Kidpower is a tapestry of many different threads woven by many different hands. Our curriculum and services have grown from the ideas, questions, teaching, feedback, and stories of countless people since I first started working on child protection, personal safety, and self-defense issues in 1985.

I want to express my appreciation to each of our Kidpower instructors, board members, honorary trustees, senior program leaders, center directors, workshop organizers, advisors, volunteers, donors, parents, students, funding partners, service partners, family members, advocates, hosts, and office staff.

Thank you for the thought, care, time, and generosity that you have given to bring Kidpower Teenpower Fullpower International to where we are today. I feel honored to have you as colleagues and as friends.

I want to give special acknowledgement to our Kidpower International Senior Program Leaders, who are highly experienced in teaching and/or organizing our programs and who have been with us for many years - and who have made significant contributions to the international organization as well as providing Kidpower services in their own communities. They include: Cornelia Baumgartner, Joe Connelly, Ellen Frankel, Amanda Golert, Angela Hamilton, Mary Jane Hayes, Jan Isaacs Henry (who is also our Featured Contributor for this new Colored Edition), Meredith Henry, Ryan Holmes, Chantal Keeney, Marylaine Léger, Erika Leonard, John Luna-Sparks, Anne Mason, Beth McGreevy, Marc Meilleur, Amy Tiemann and Maria Gisella Gámez.

Our Board of Directors includes the following deeply committed people who provide significant support to our organization: April Yee, Board President; Kim Leisey, Vice President; Peter Lewis, Treasurer; Penny Campbell Loftesness, Secretary; and members: Abby Bleistein, Claire Laughlin, Ellen Frankel, Dave Harrison, Arnie Kamrin, Rich Kamrin, Maryse Postelwaite, John Luna-Sparks, Jennifer Turner-Davis, Julie Shattuck, and Zaida Torres.

And, THANK YOU to Timothy Dunphy, who is our Kidpower International Program Co-Founder, for partnering with me in our early years to create our original programs that are the foundation of our work in ways that are effective, empowering, and FUN! – and for continuing to help bring Kidpower out into the world as a member of our training team.

Finally, I want to honor the memory of our long-time supporter, mentor, and former Board President Nancy Driscoll, whose wisdom and generosity have helped and keep helping Kidpower grow from a good idea into a great reality!

Take a look at our Annual Reports and History on our kidpower.org website to learn more about these people and the many other remarkable people who are working together to further Kidpower's vision of helping to create cultures of safety, respect, and kindness for everyone, everywhere.

Writing each person's story would be a book unto itself!

About Our Author

Irene van der Zande is the Founder and Executive Director of Kidpower Teenpower Fullpower International. Since 1989, Irene's talented leadership and collaboration have earned Kidpower an outstanding reputation worldwide for developing, organizing, and presenting high quality child protection, positive communication, advocacy, self-defense, and personal safety programs and curriculums for everyone, everywhere.

She is a proven expert at adapting Kidpower's services and programs to meet the needs of those facing increased risks of bullying, abuse, and violence because of difficult life challenges such as disabilities, poverty, and prejudice.

Irene is the co-author of the best-selling book, *Doing Right by Our Kids: Protecting Child Safety at All Levels*, which features Kidpower skills and principles as well as other best practices. As Kidpower's expert lead author, Irene places time-tested life-saving social-emotional skills and lessons directly into the hands of parents and professionals through her numerous books, articles, and other educational resources.

She is an inspiring, passionate, and entertaining speaker, trainer, and storyteller who is a master at preparing people to transform problems into successful practices; to take charge of their safety and well-being; and to develop joyful relationships that enrich their lives.

About Our Illustrator

Amanda Golert is an experienced self-defense instructor, trainer, passionate advocate for personal safety for children and other vulnerable people, the Center Director of Kidpower Sweden—and she also likes to draw!

Since 1999, Amanda has supported the growth and development of Kidpower Teenpower Fullpower International. She works in partnership with Irene to illustrate, edit, and design the Kidpower cartoon books and many other educational materials.

In 2004, Irene was looking for someone who could draw the pictures she had in her head for our Kidpower curriculum - and she found Amanda! Since then, Amanda's keen eye, dry humor, skilled hands, and deep understanding of our work have led to our creation of educational materials that have helped millions of children, teens, and adults all over the world learn how to have more fun and fewer problems with people.

About Our Featured Contributor

Special thanks to Jan Isaacs Henry, our Kidpower Colorado Center Director and Kidpower Teenpower International Senior Program Leader, for inspiring, supporting, and editing this new color edition of our *Kidpower Children's Safety Comics*. Jan is a former psychotherapist who specialized in the treatment of abuse and trauma. Since starting the Colorado Center in 1994, Jan's contributions have greatly increased the quality and scope of our programs and curriculum.